"Through the act of drawing, children can cultivate their imagination, enhance their ability to solve problems, and bolster their sense of self-assurance." —

Kait Arciuolo
Founder
Learn & Grow
TKTCollection

Copyright ©April 2023 TKTCollection Publishing.

I Can Draw - Animal Faces
LEFT HANDED EDITION
Learn and Grow Art Vol.1

Independently Published By:

TKTCollection
ISBN:978-1-959247-18-0

April 2023

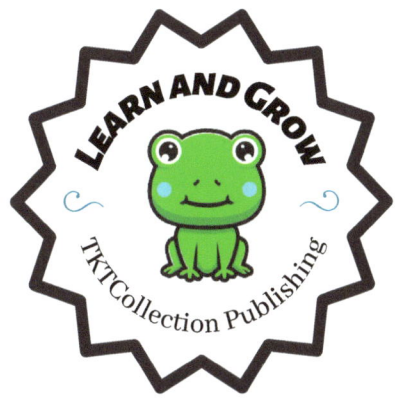

Copyright © April 2023 TKTCollection, Learn and Grow. All Rights Reserved. No part of the publication may be used or reproduced, distributed, or transmitted, in any form or by any means, including photocopying, recording, or other electronic or mechanical methods, without the publisher's written permission tktcollection.com

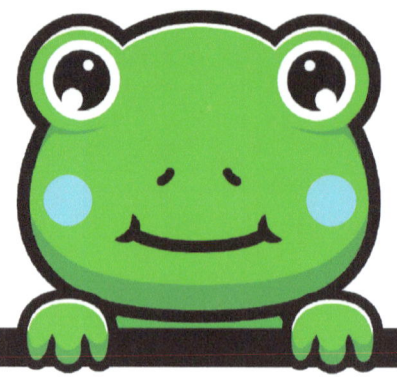

THIS LEARN AND GROW BOOK BELONGS TO:

_____

I Can Draw - Animal Faces
LEFT HANDED EDITION

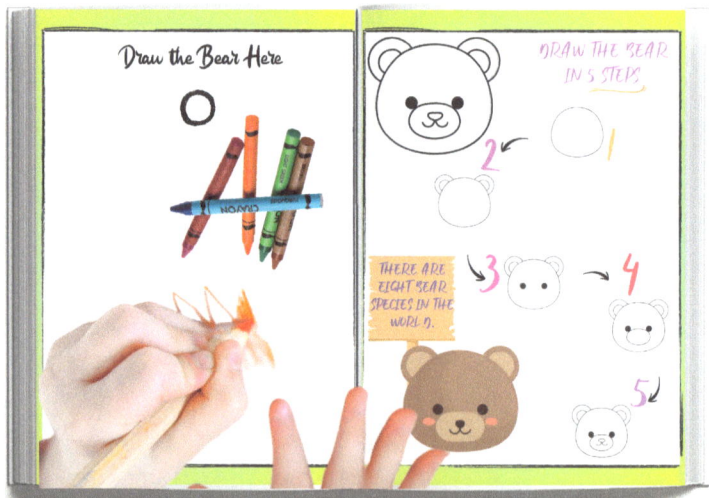

Scan here for more great Learn and Grow Books on Amazon

Kids. Ask Your Grown Up First!

Before we get started, you'll need a few things

- Lead or Mechanical Pencil to draw your picture.
- Eraser in case you want to make any corrections.

(You can use colored pencils, markers to color when your done!)

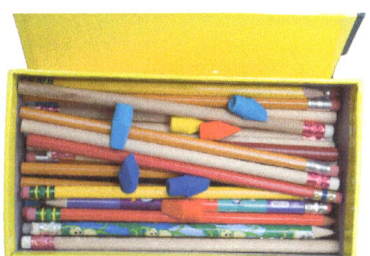 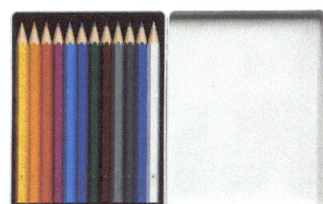

You will find your Drawing Space on the Left page and your Instructions on the Right.

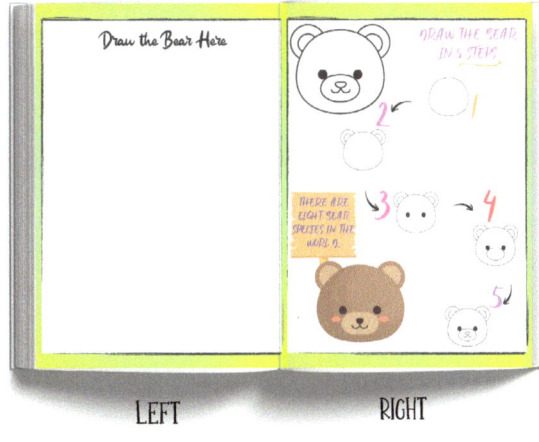

LEFT   RIGHT

This page is for you to drawn your picture.

Step-By-Step Instructions that break down the drawing into just 5 or 6 steps.

Each Parts builds on the previous step, Just take it step-by-step, and remember, to enjoy practicing!

Draw the Horse Here

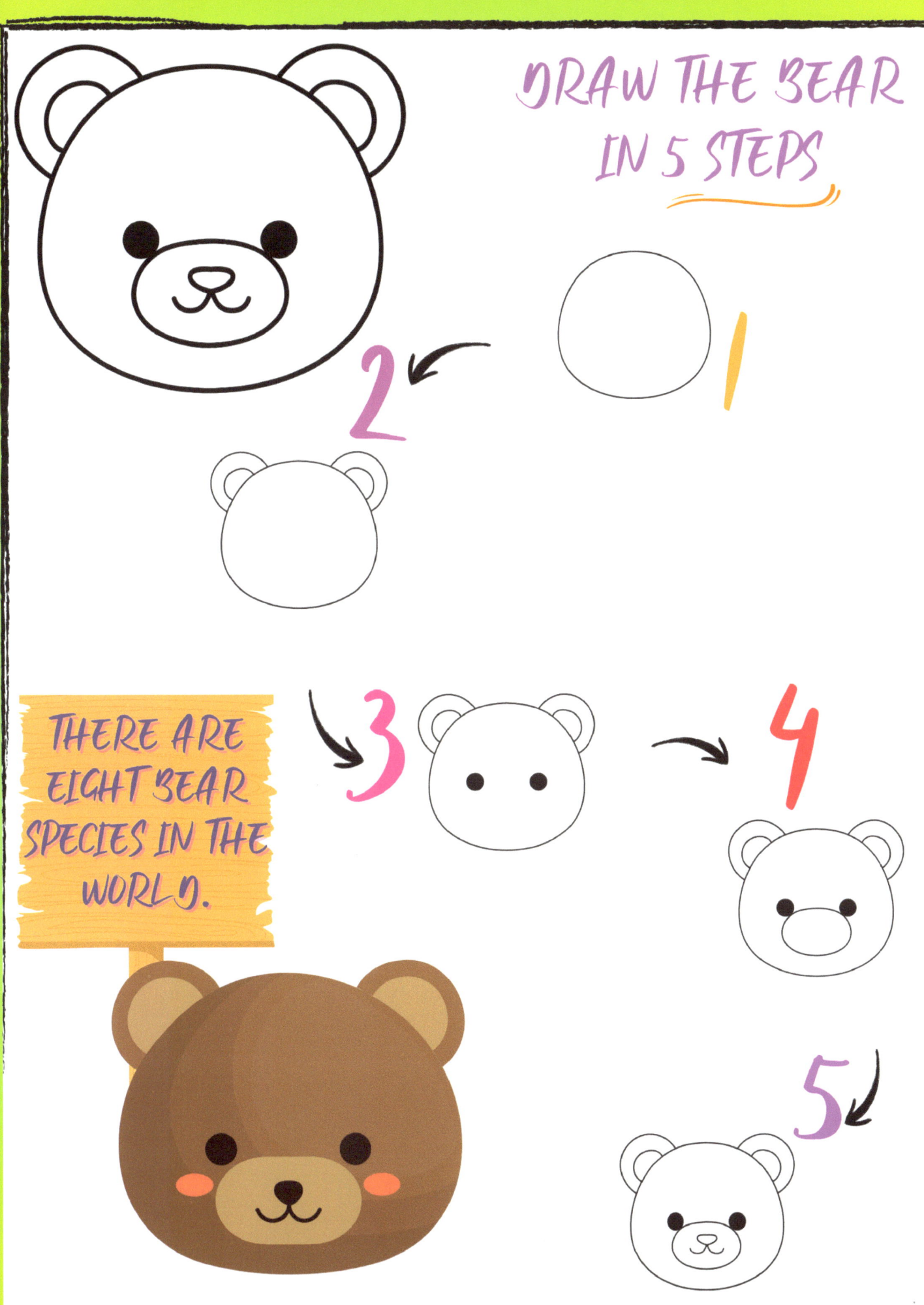

Draw the Bear Here

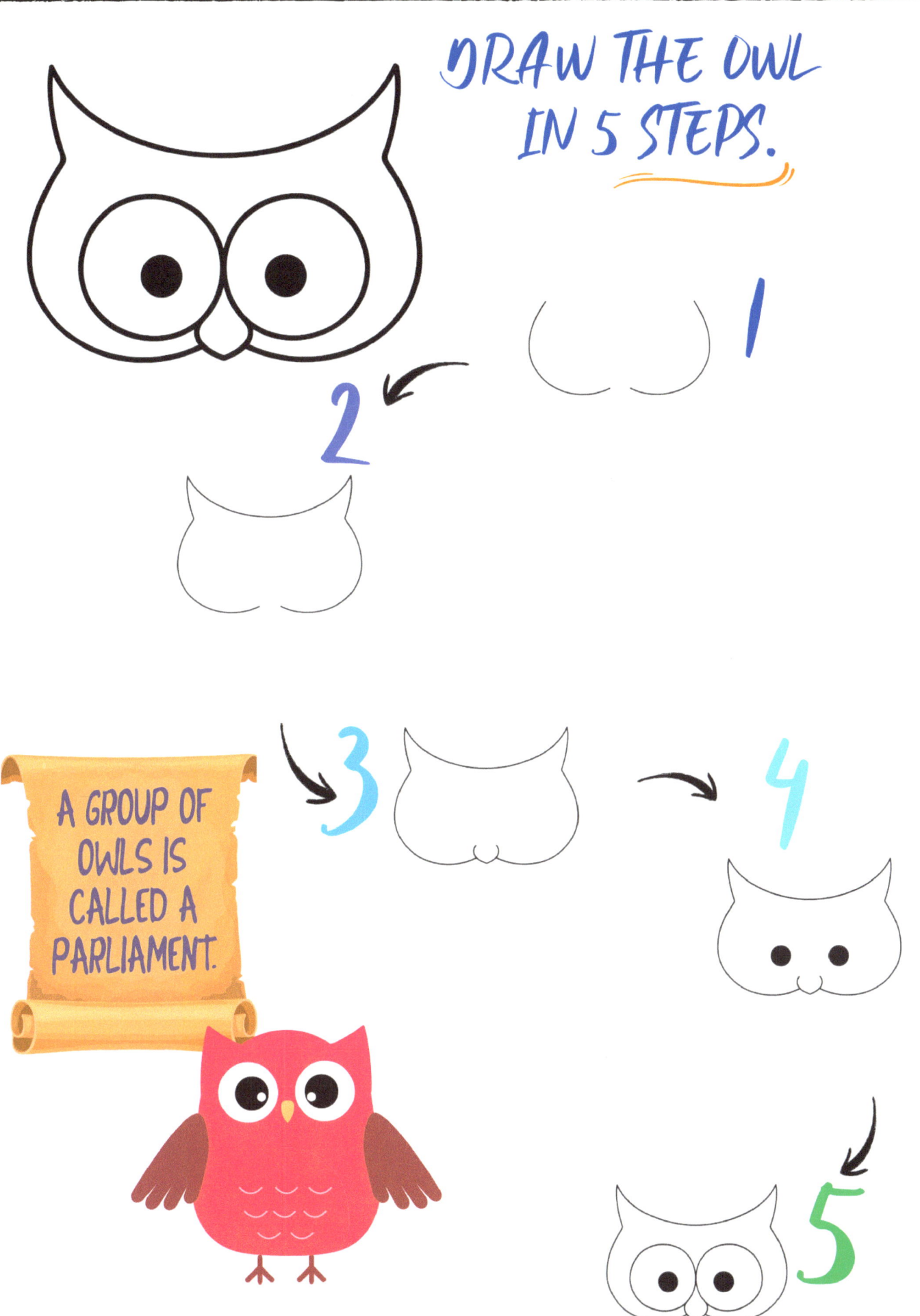

Draw the Owl Here

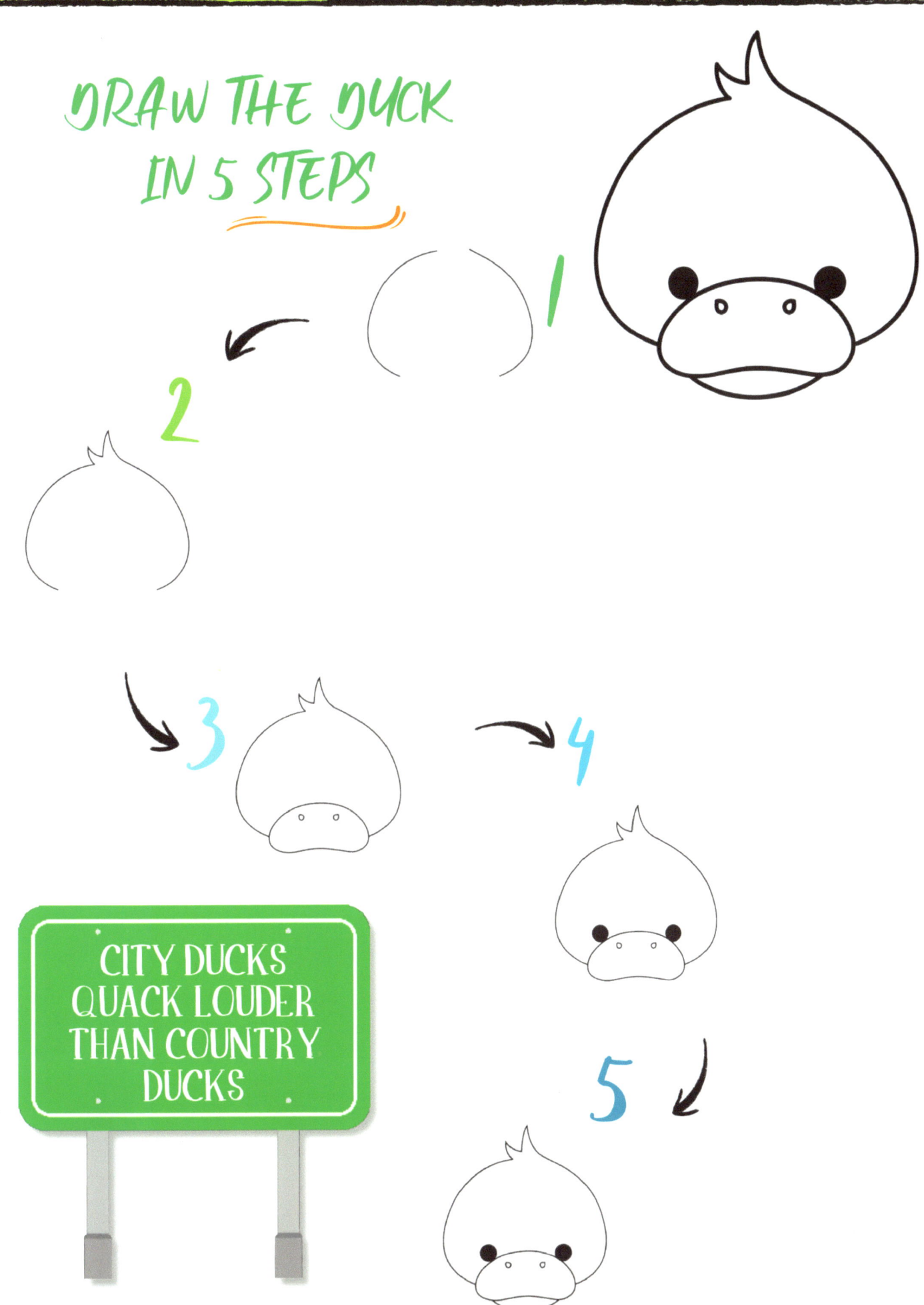

Draw the Duck Here

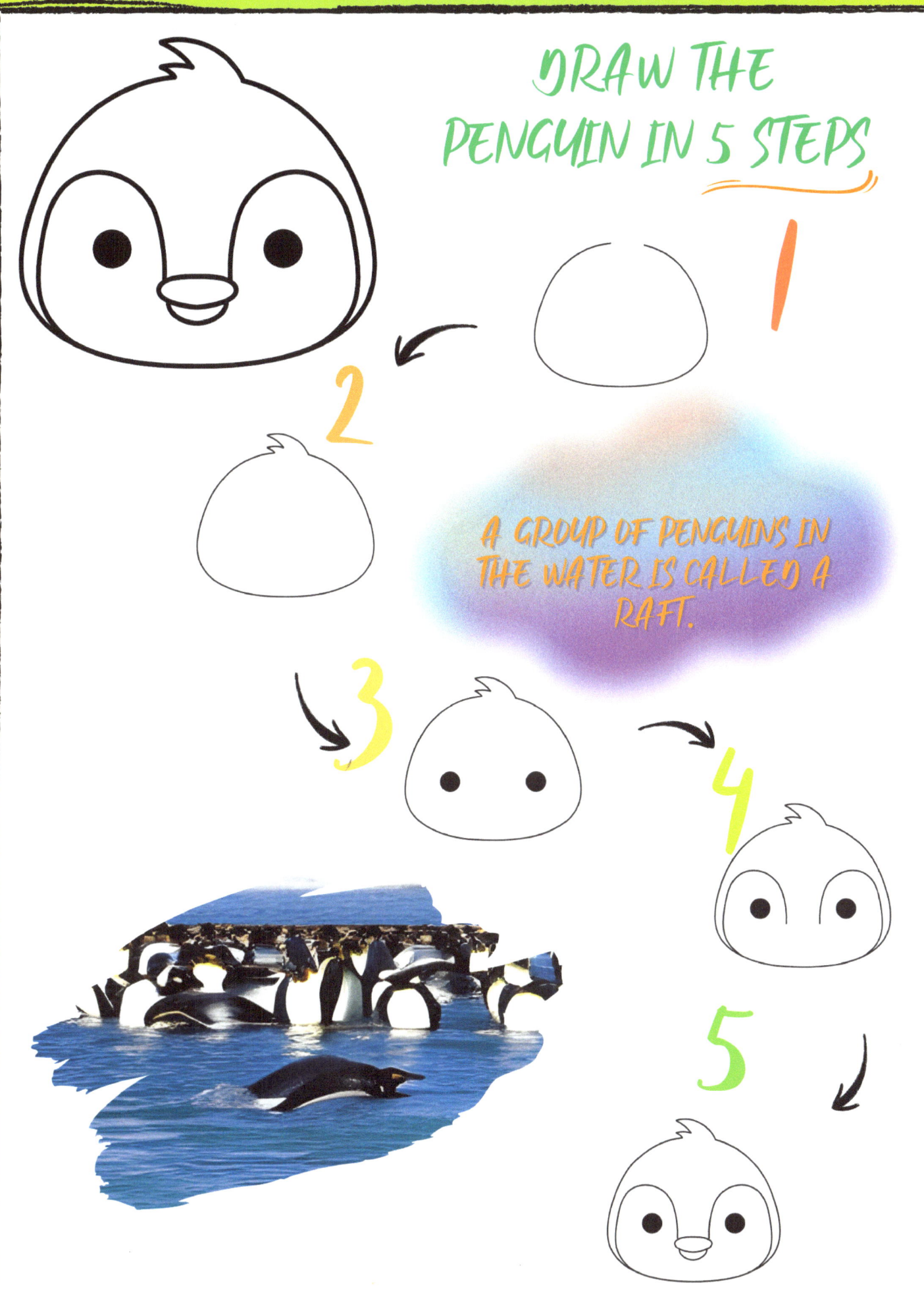

Draw the Penguin Here

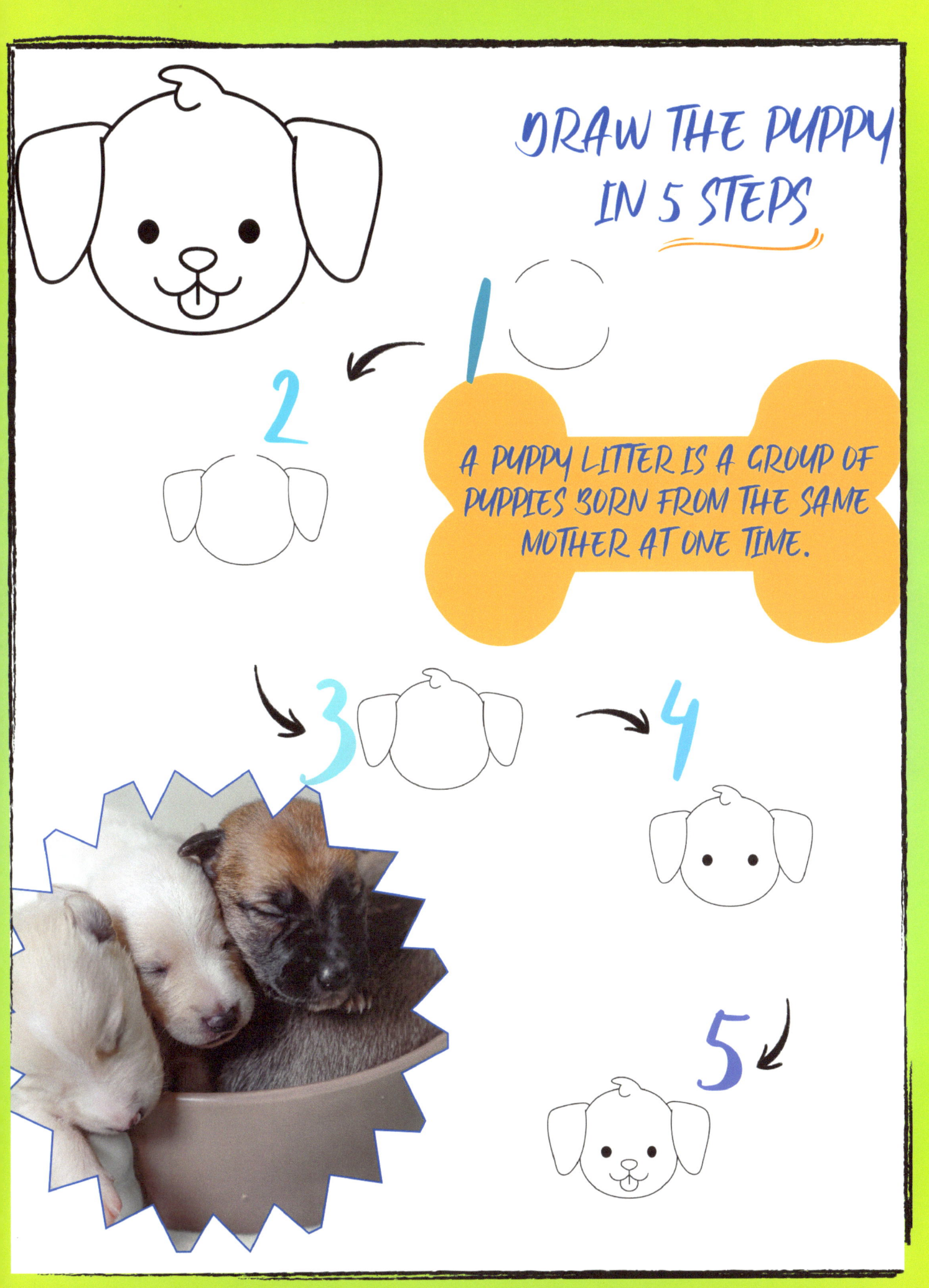

Draw the Puppy Here

DRAW THE BUNNY IN 6 STEPS

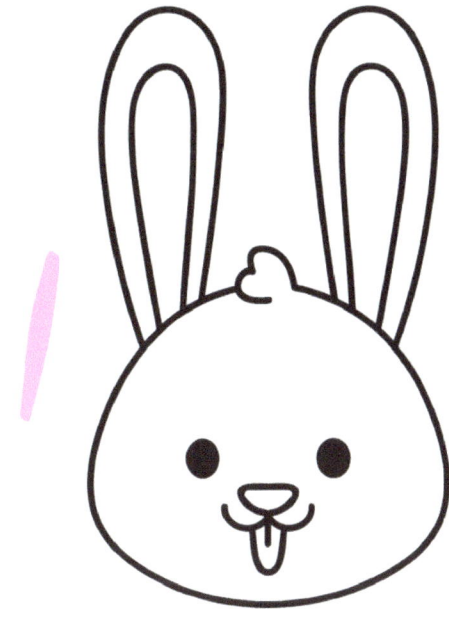

1

2

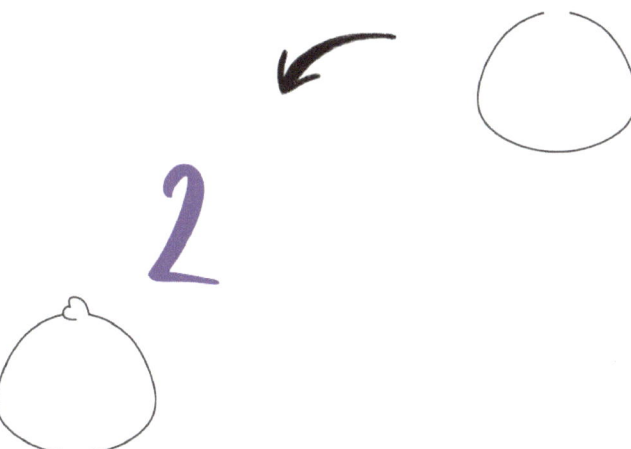

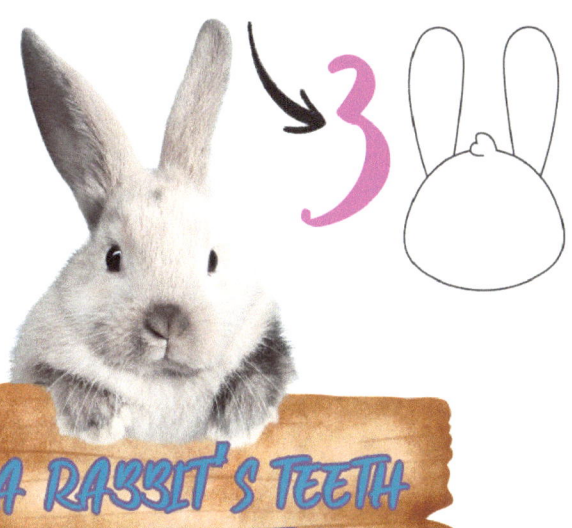

3

4

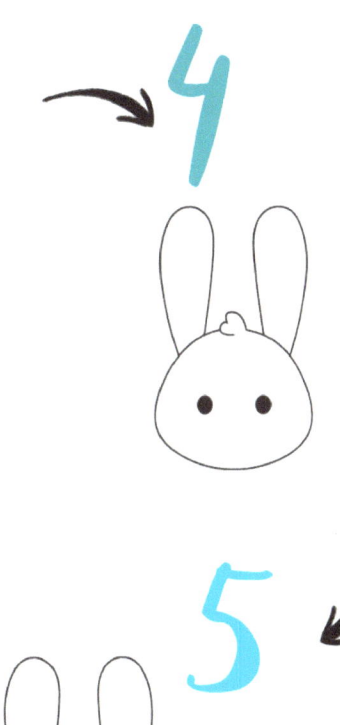

A RABBIT'S TEETH NEVER STOP GROWING

5

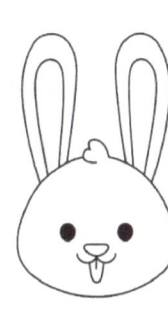

6

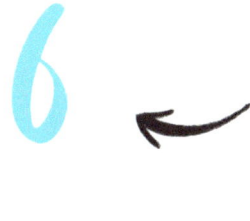

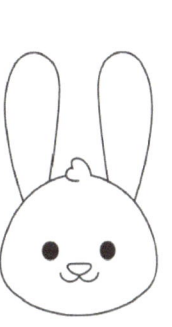

Draw the Rabbit Here

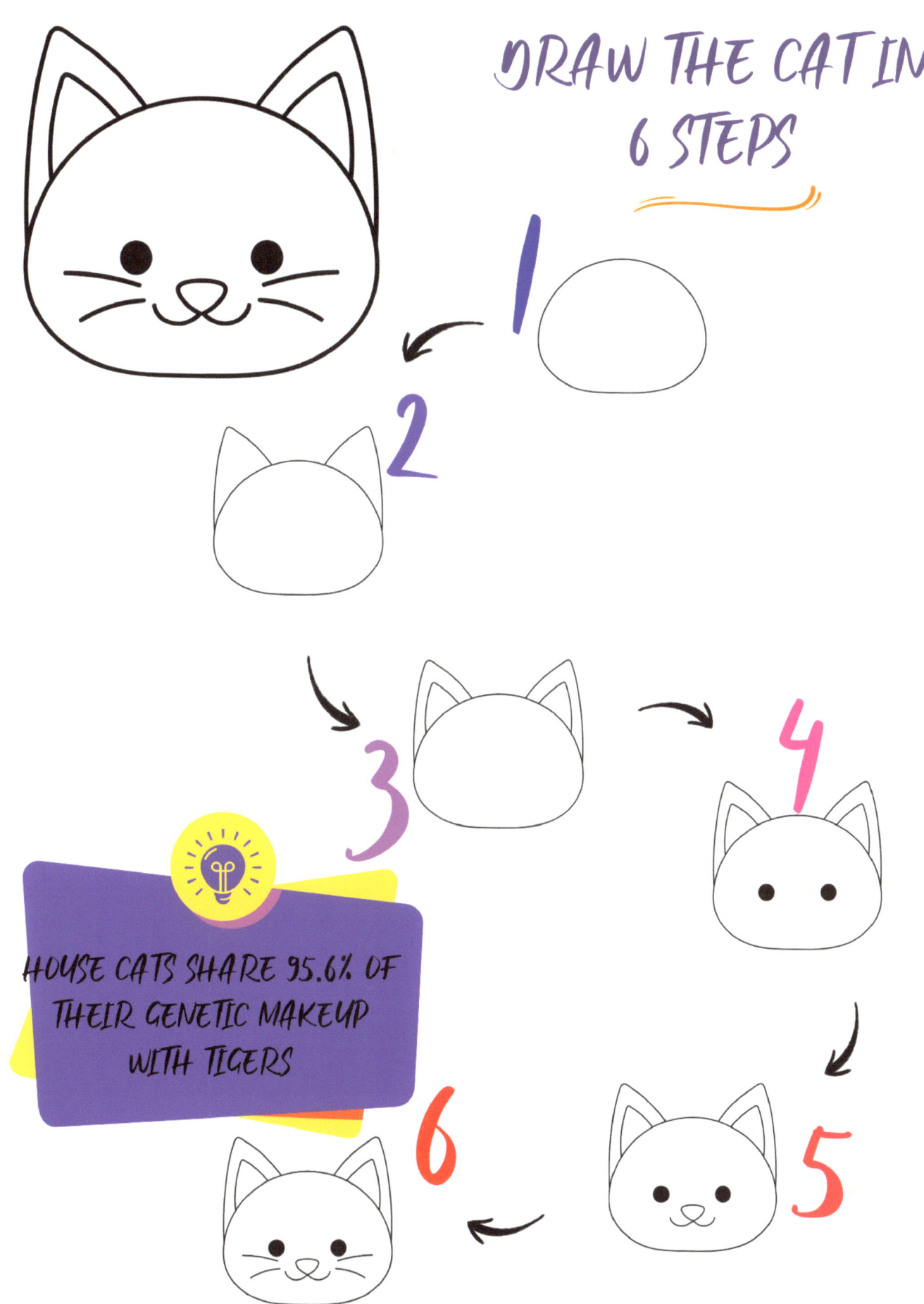

DRAW THE CAT IN 6 STEPS

HOUSE CATS SHARE 95.6% OF THEIR GENETIC MAKEUP WITH TIGERS

Draw the Cat Here

DRAW THE ROOSTER IN 6 STEPS

1
2
3
4
5
6

YOU DO NOT NEED A ROOSTER TO HAVE CHICKEN EGGS.

Draw the Rooster Here

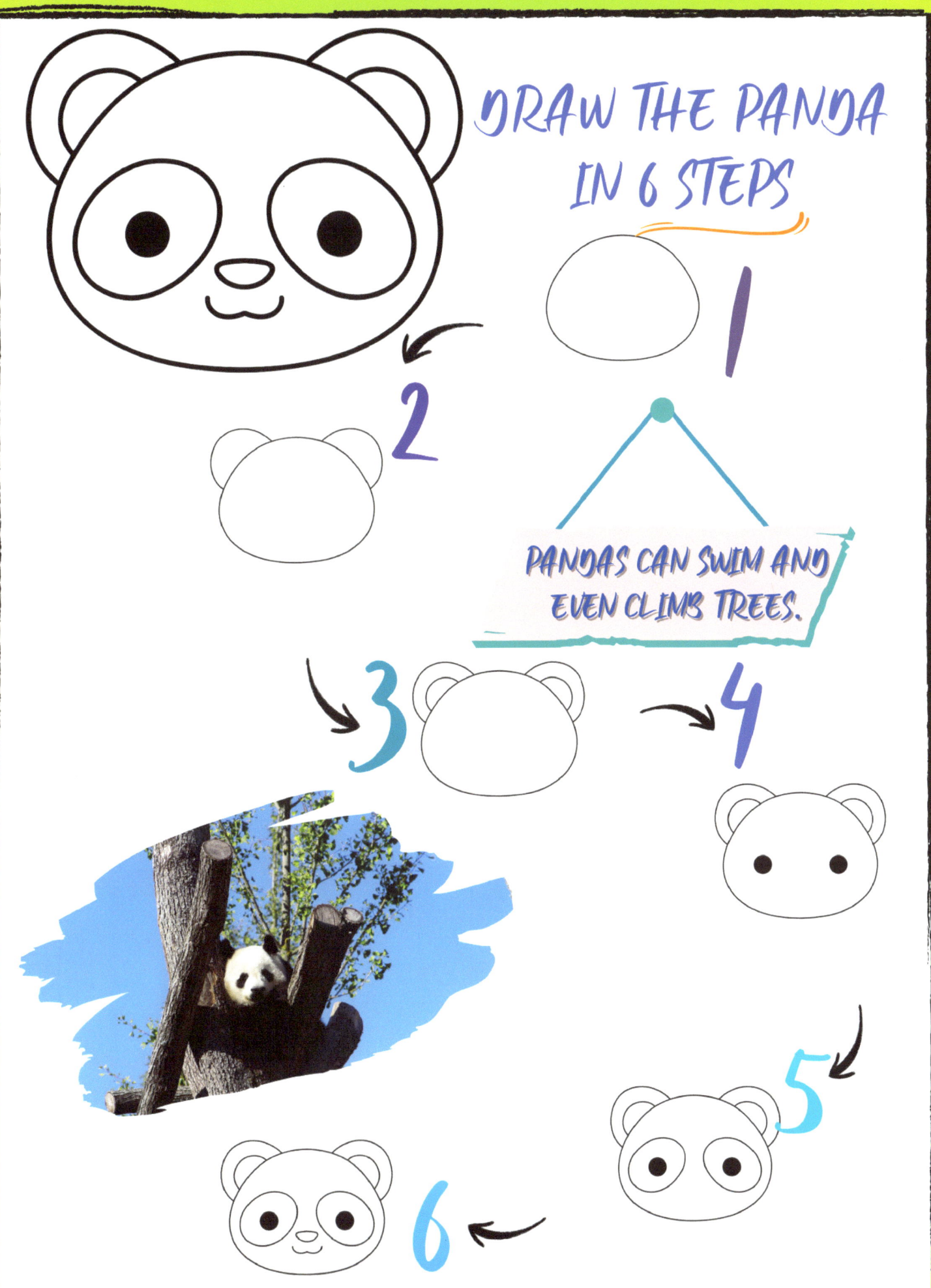

Draw the Panda Here

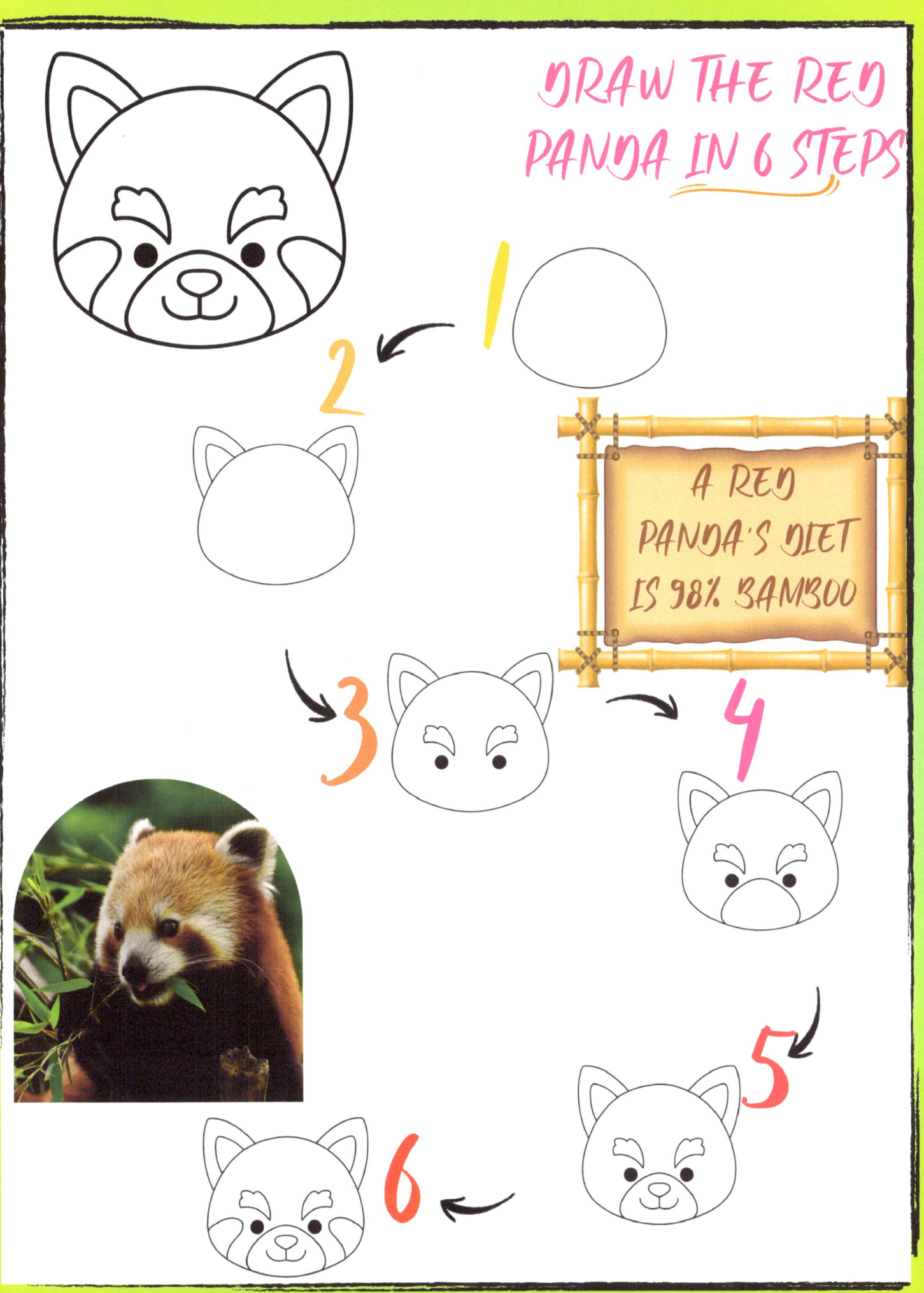

Draw the Red Panda Here

DRAW THE MULE IN 6 STEPS

1
2
3
4
5
6

MULES HAVE HARDER HOOVES THAN HORSES WHICH MAKES THEM GREAT FOR ROCKY TERRAIN

Draw the Mule Here

DRAW THE TIGER IN 6 STEPS

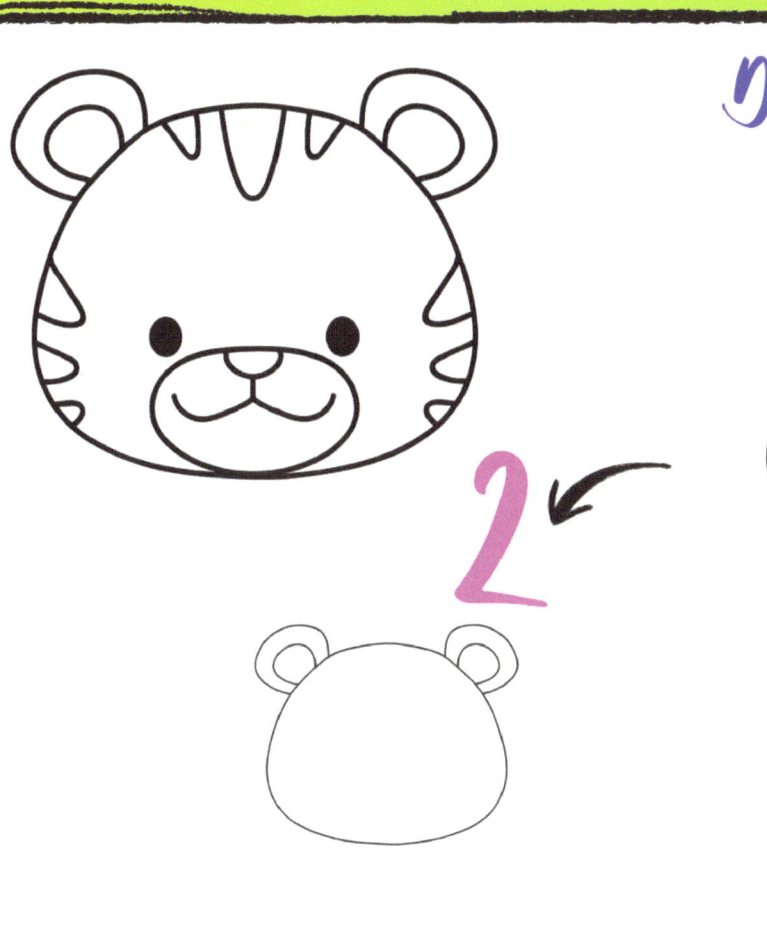
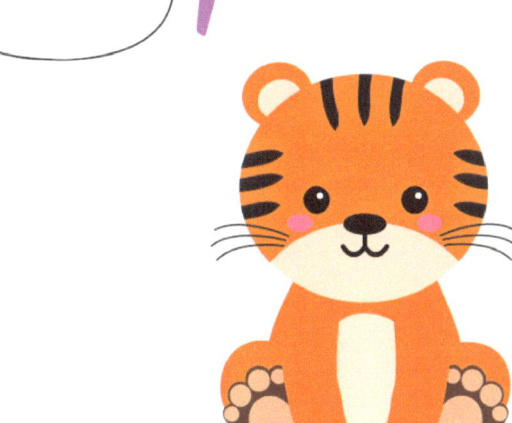
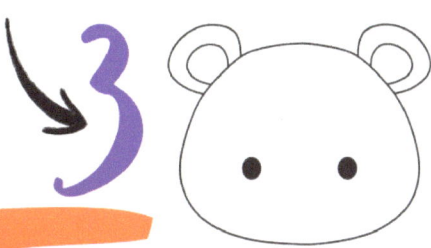
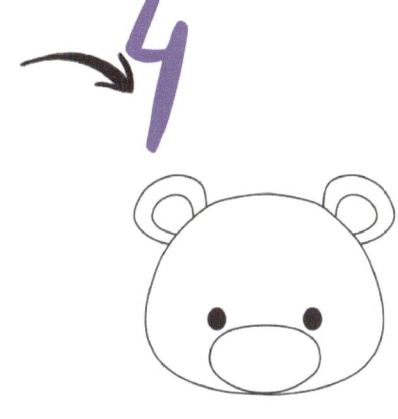

PATTERN OF STRIPES IS AS UNIQUE AS A HUMAN FINGERPRINT – NO TWO TIGERS HAVE IDENTICAL COATS.

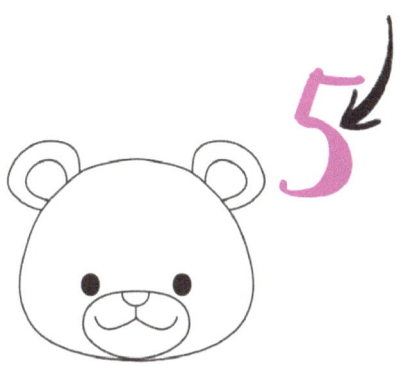
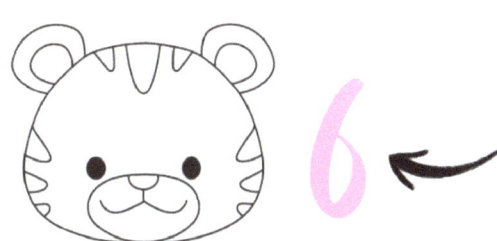

Draw the Tiger Here

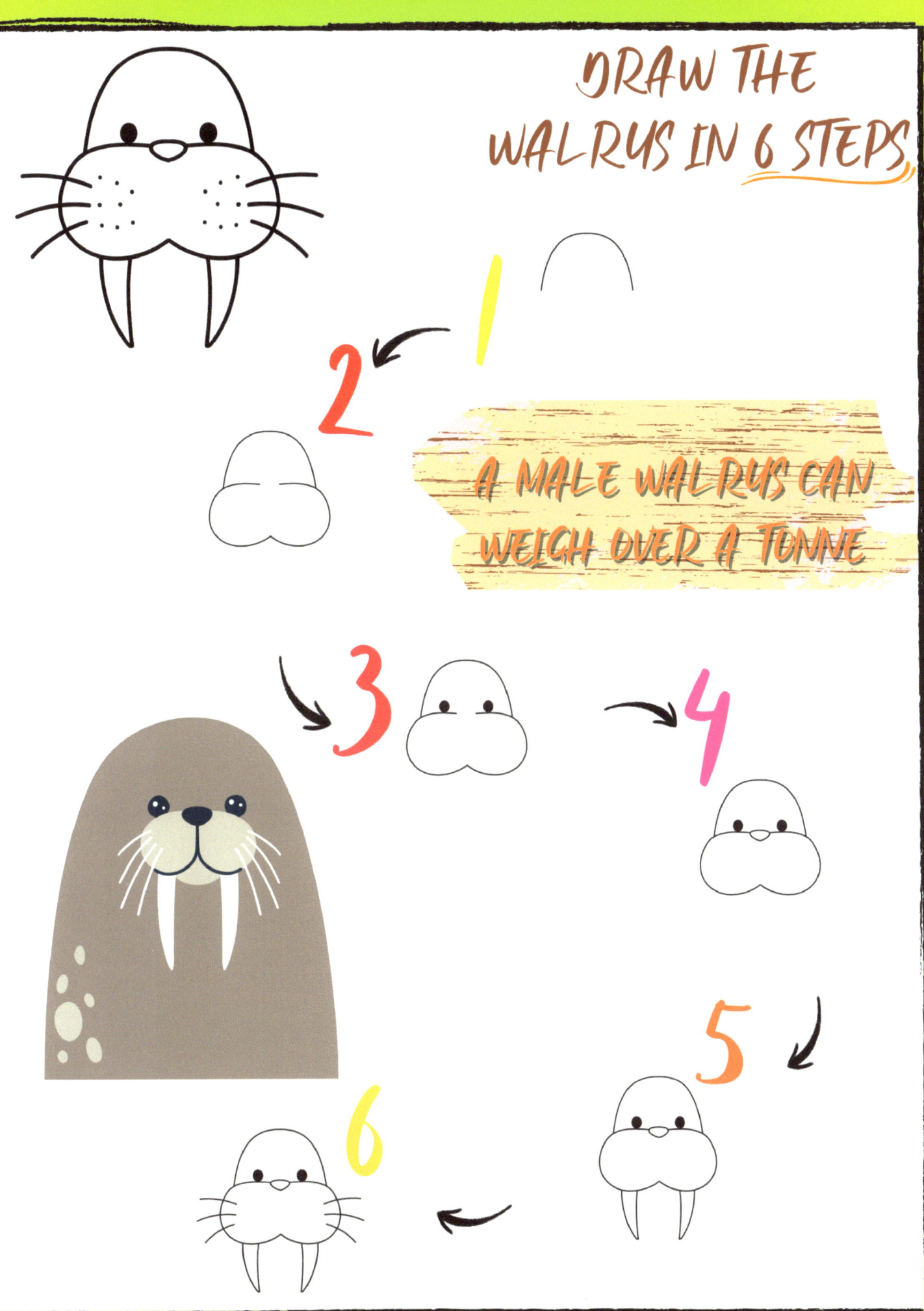

Draw the Walrus Here

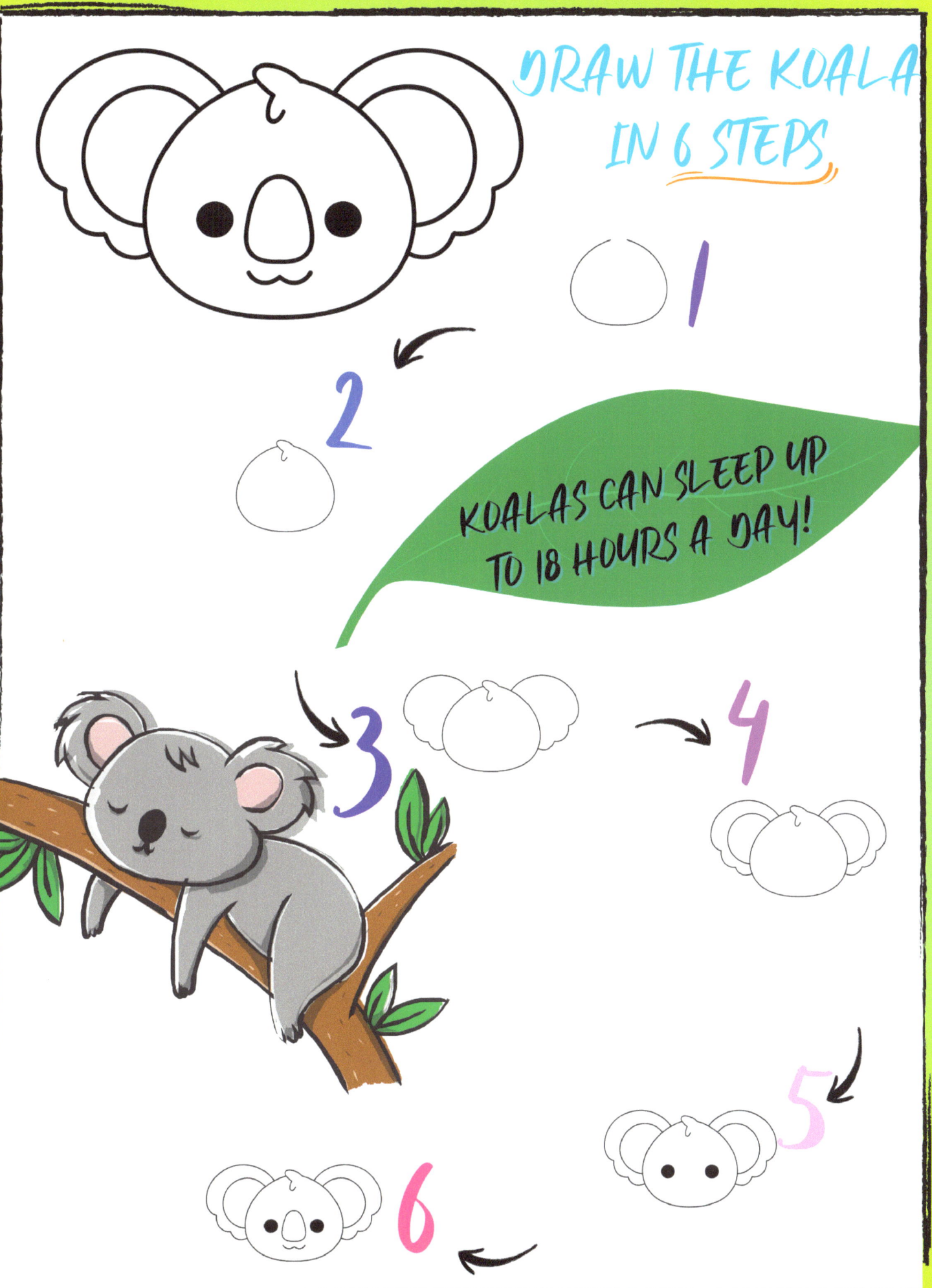

Draw the Koala Here

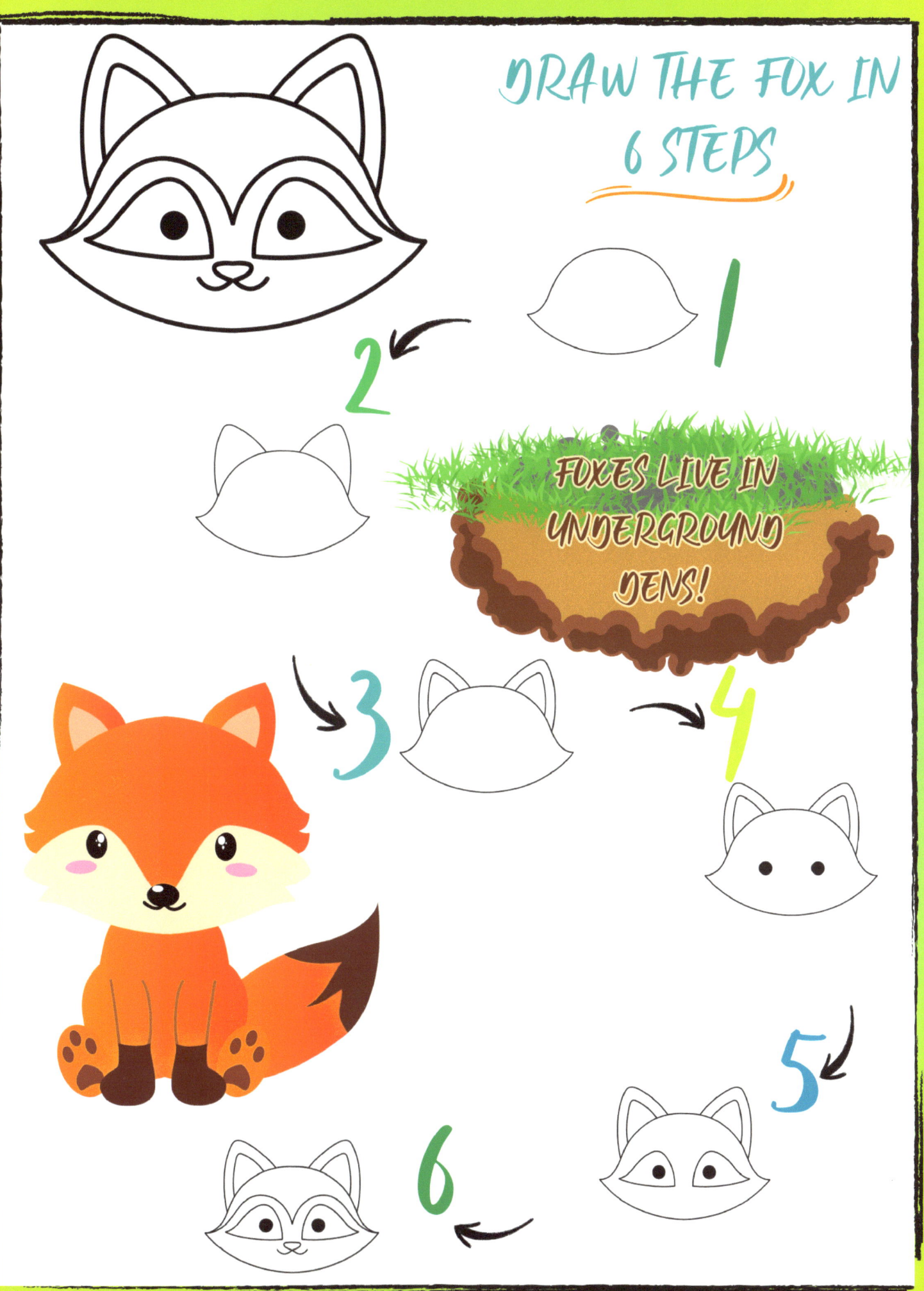

Draw the Fox Here

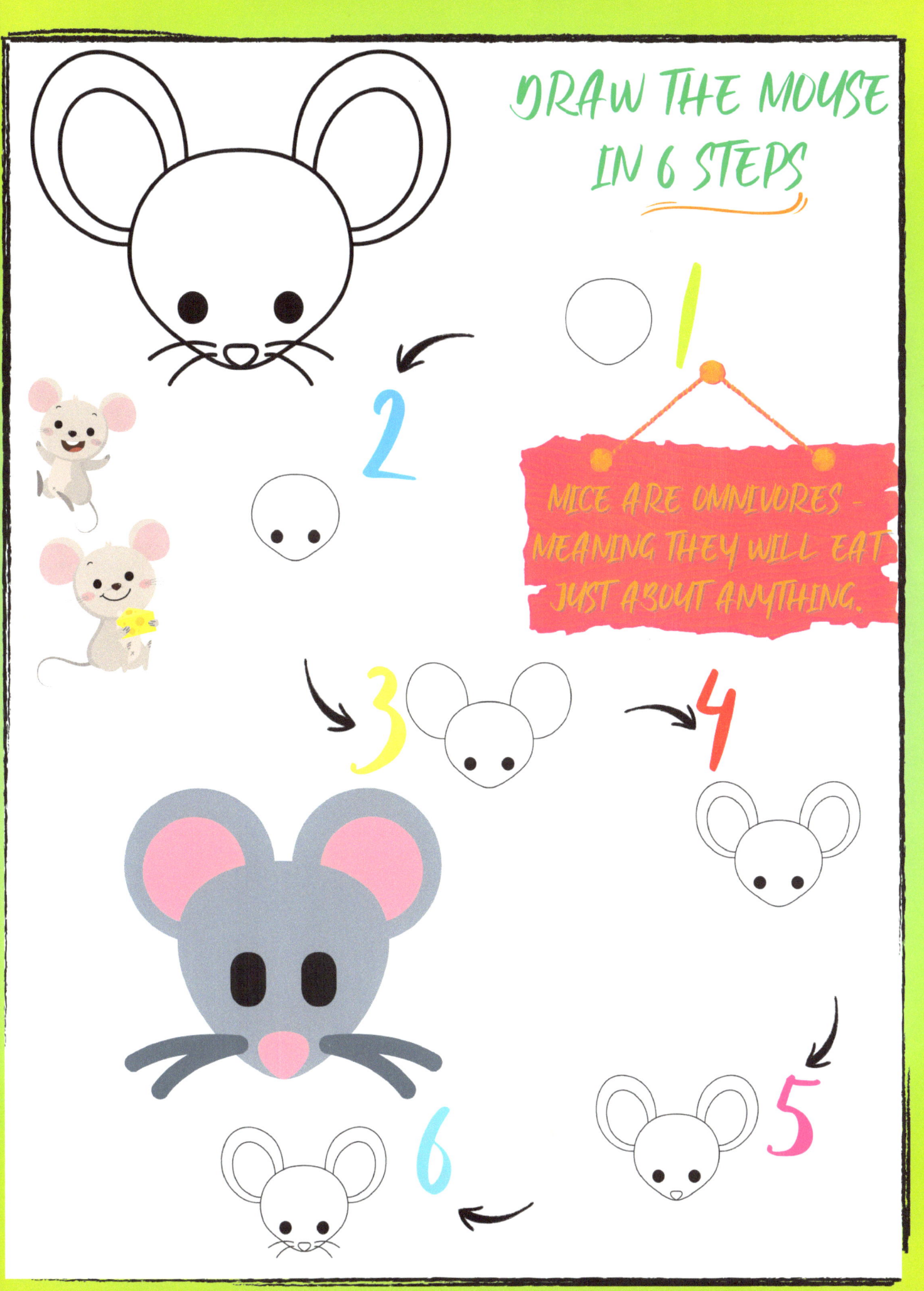

Draw the Mouse Here

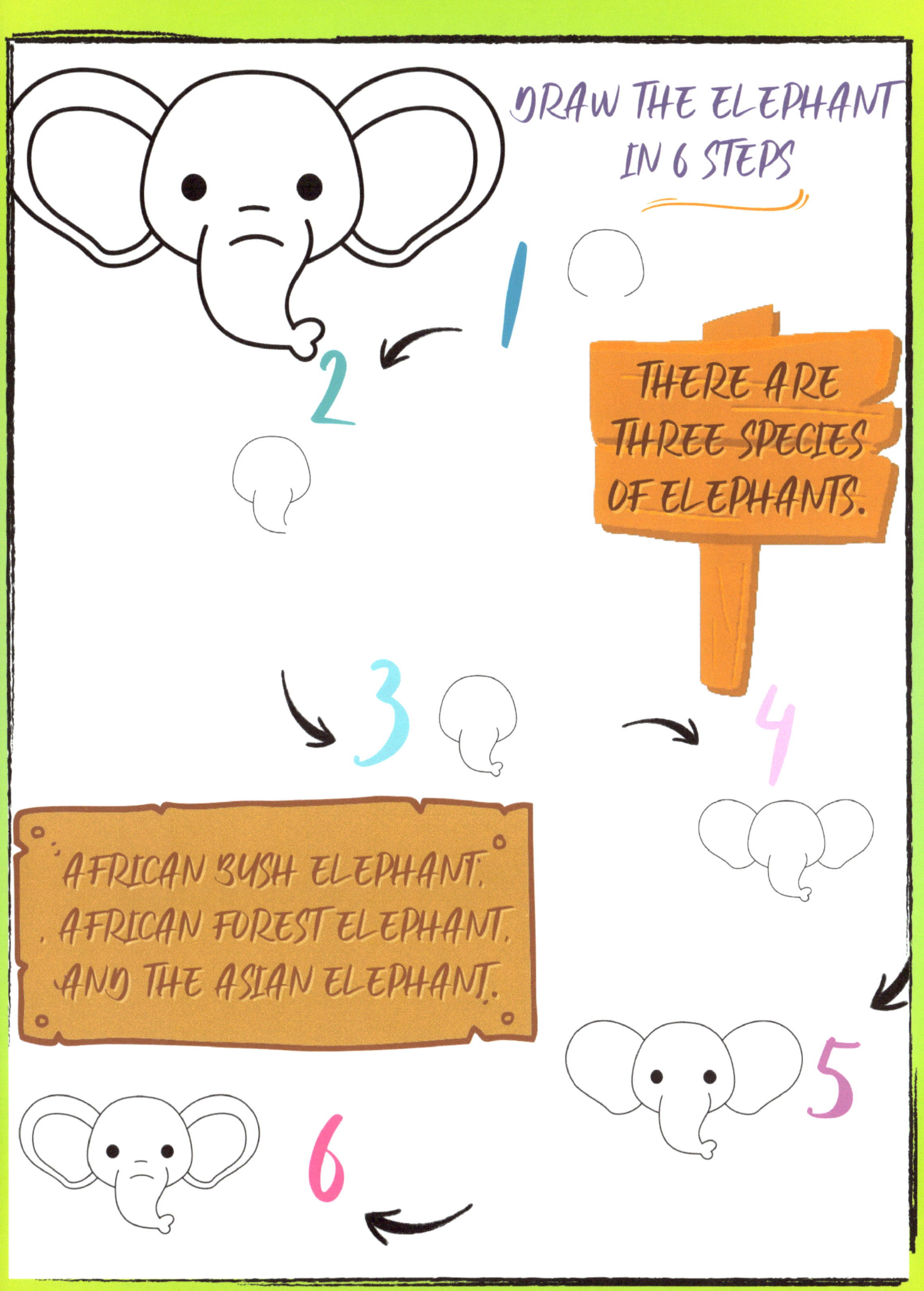

Draw the Elephant Here

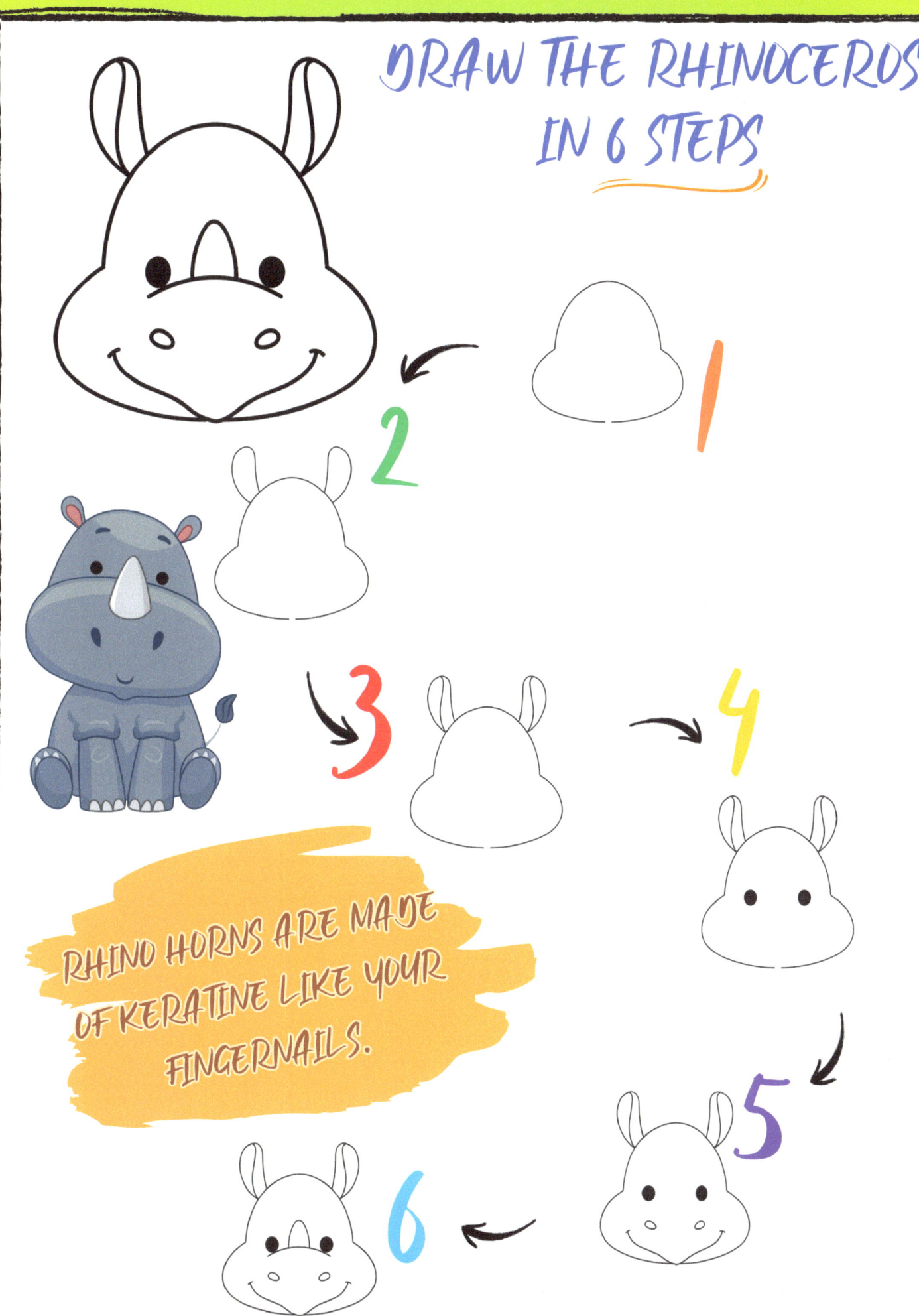

Draw the Rhinoceros Here

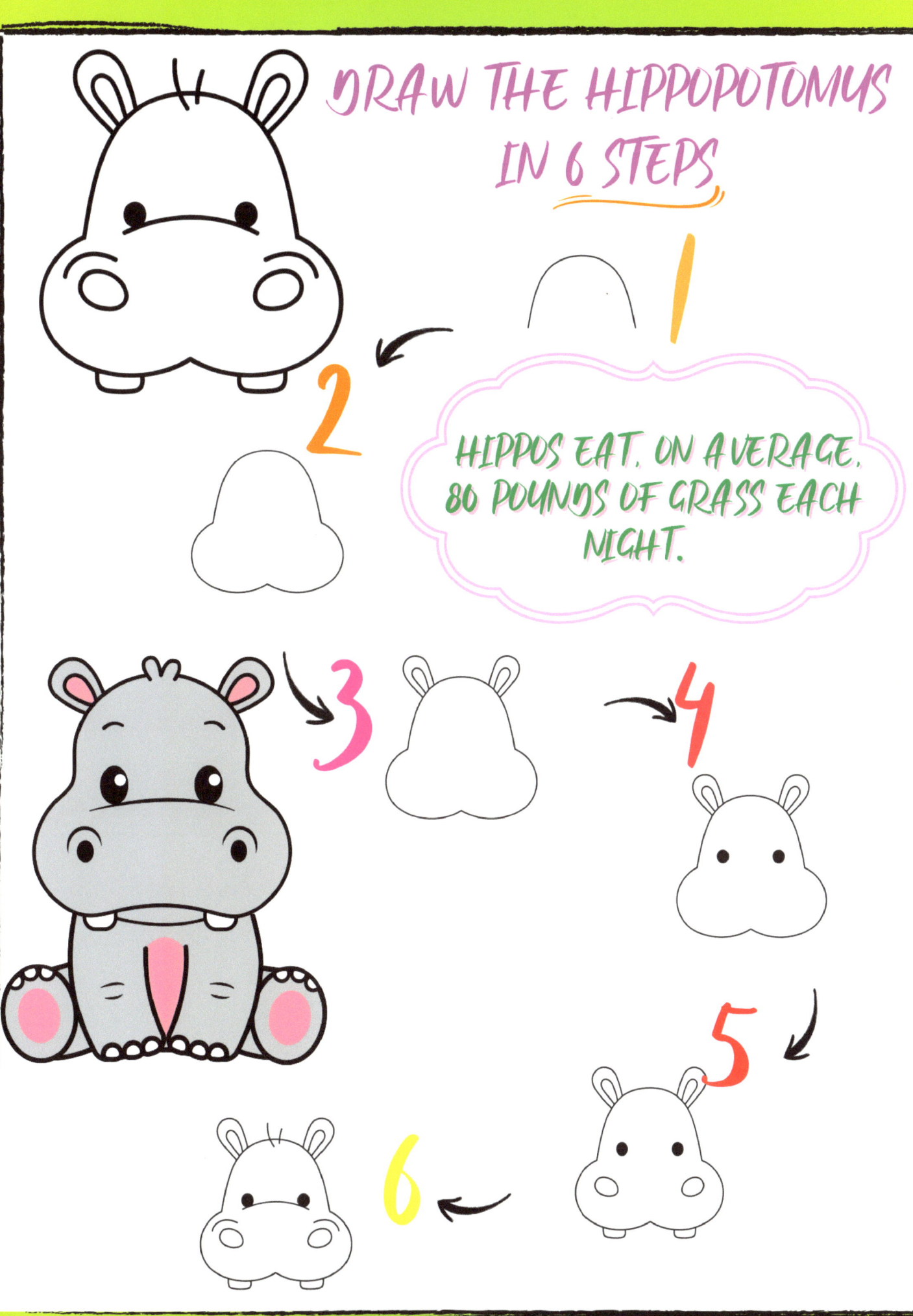

Draw the Hippopotamus Here

DRAW THE HORSE IN 6 STEPS.

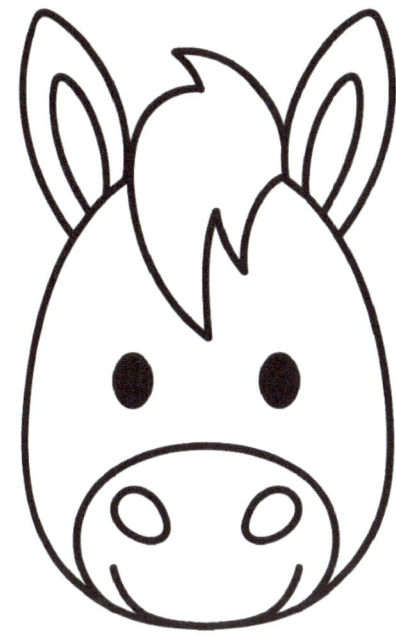

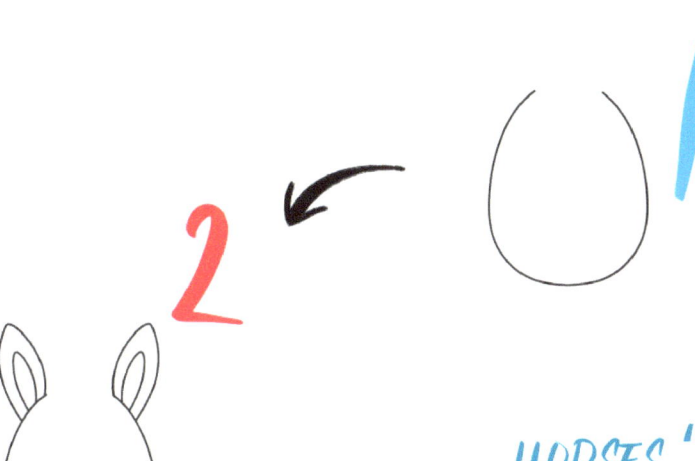

HORSES "LOCK" THEIR LEGS TO AVOID COLLAPSING WHILE SLEEPING STANDING UP

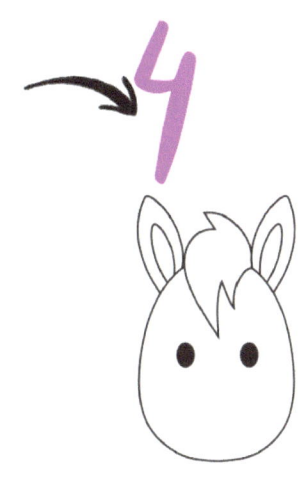

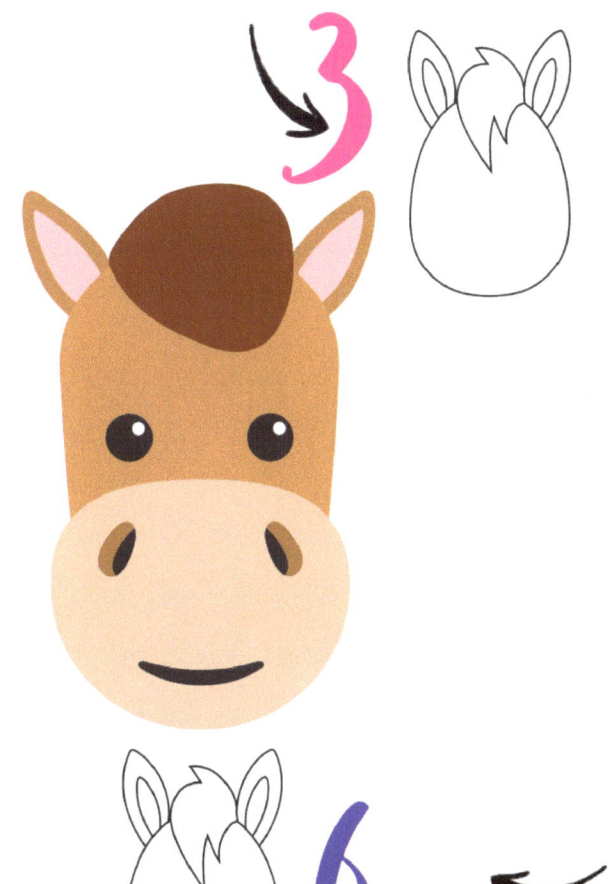

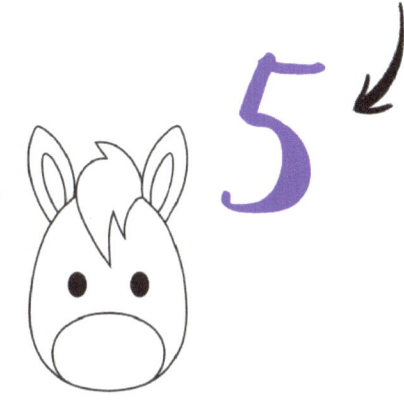

Kids, Ask Your Grown Up Before Scanning Download, or Signing Up For Anything First!

WANT FREE COLORING PAGES?

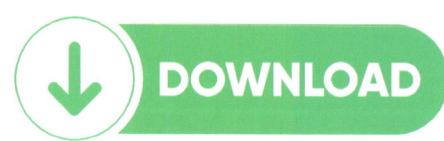

TKTCollection Freebies Page
Download Free Coloring Pages, Puzzles and More!

SCAN ME!

Sign up for the TKTCollection
SCAN ME!
Newsletter Here.

SCAN HERE FOR MORE
LEARN & GROW
BOOKS ON AMAZON!

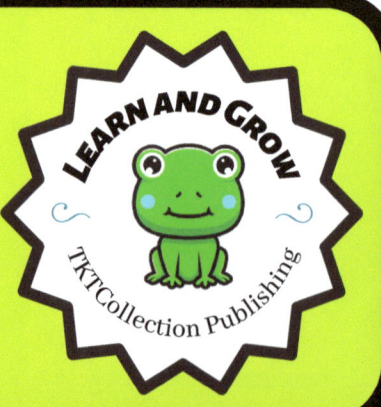

www.ingramcontent.com/pod-product-compliance
Lightning Source LLC
Chambersburg PA
CBHW040413220526
45473CB00004B/1223